I0414033

Giraffes Coloring Book
60 Easy Zentangle Giraffe Designs with Paisley and Mandala Style Patterns for Stress Relief
and Relaxation

By Peaceful Mind Adult Coloring Books

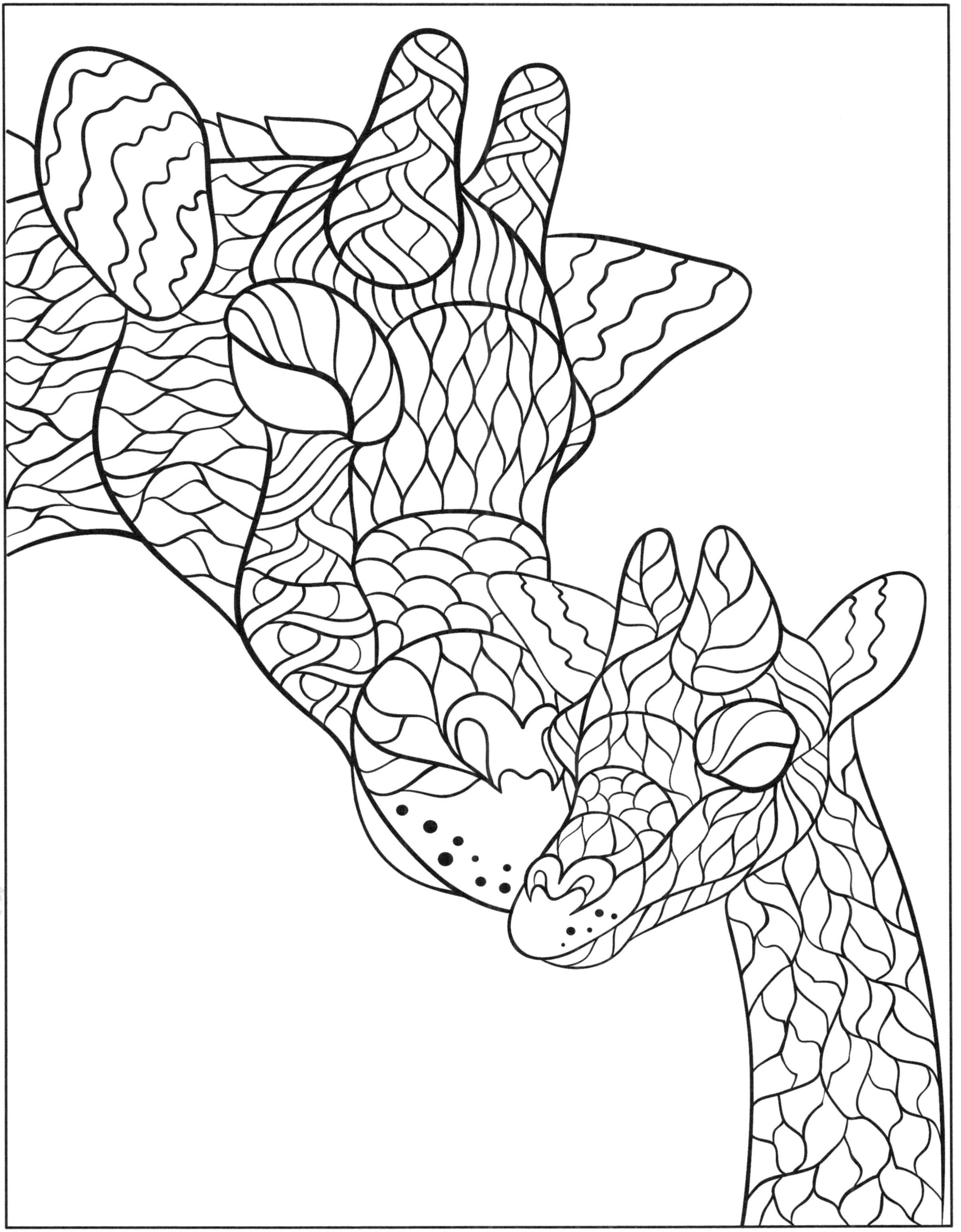

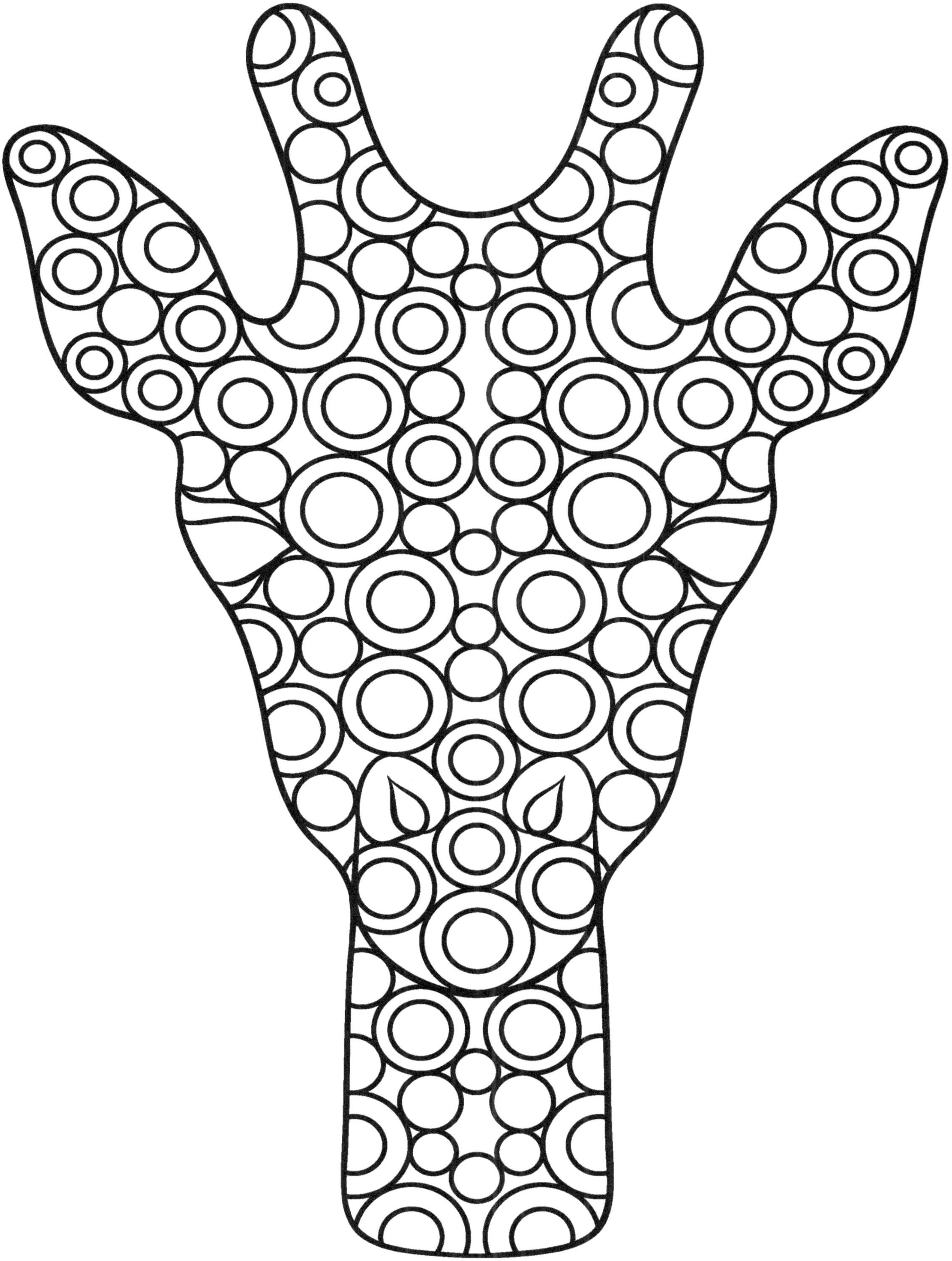

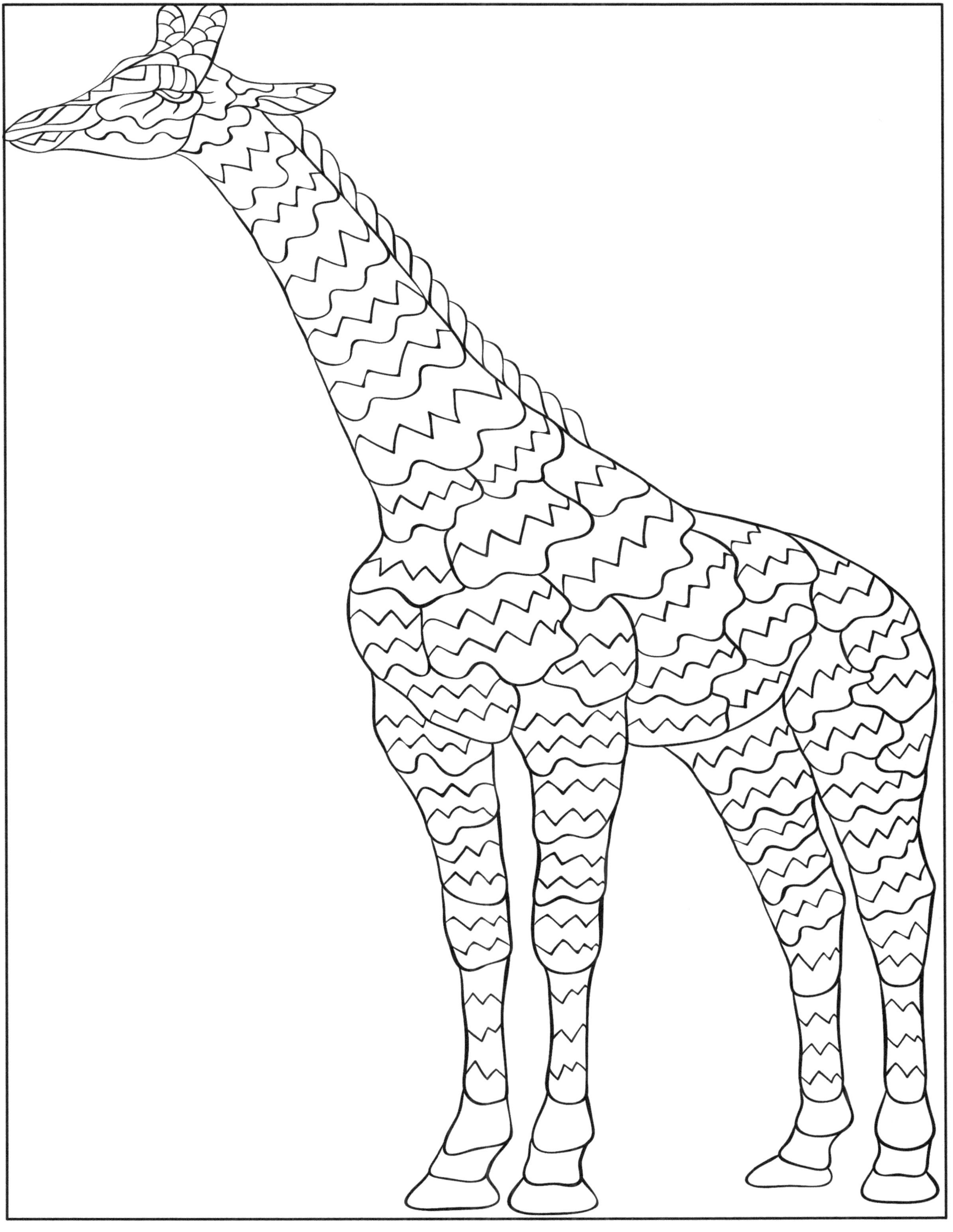

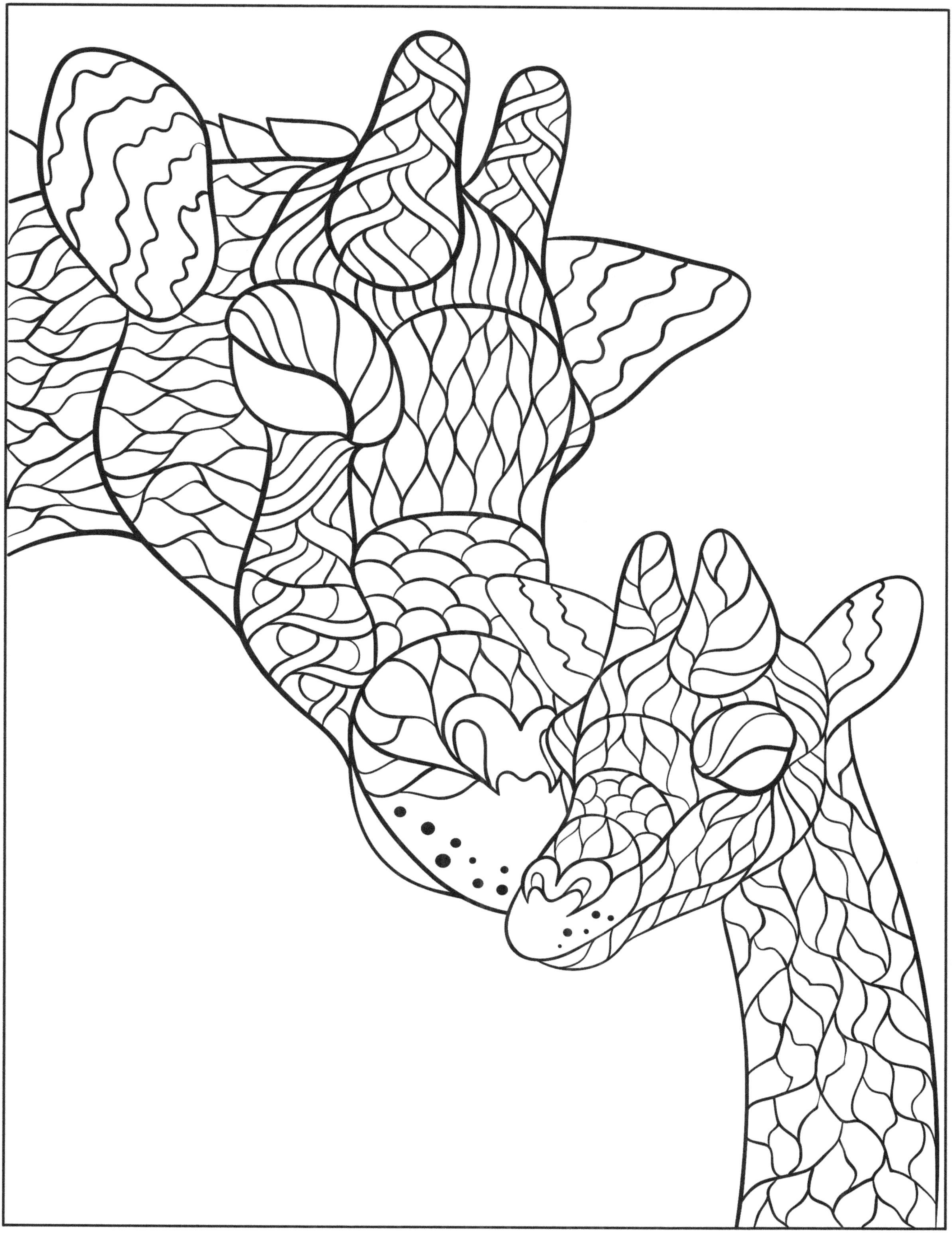

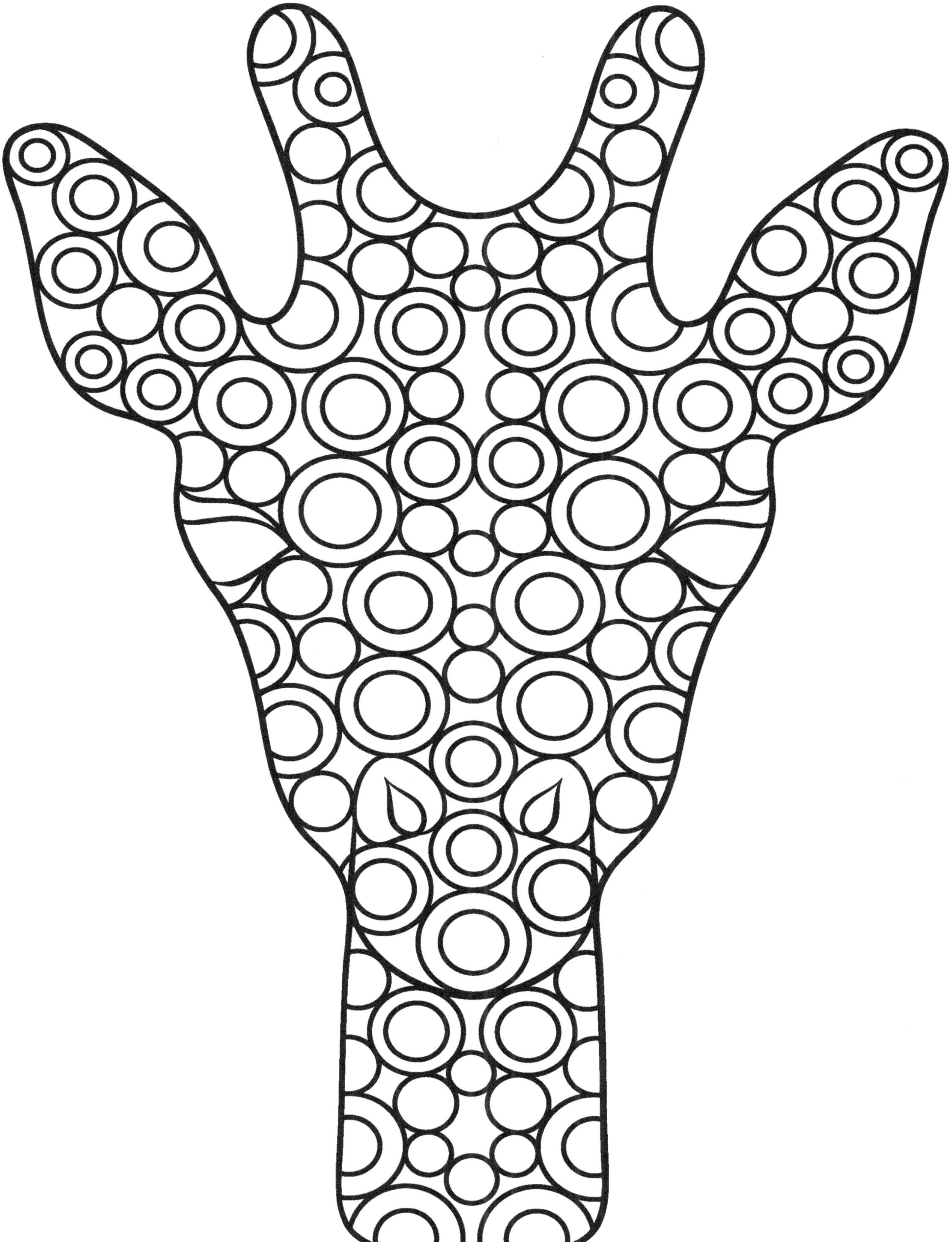

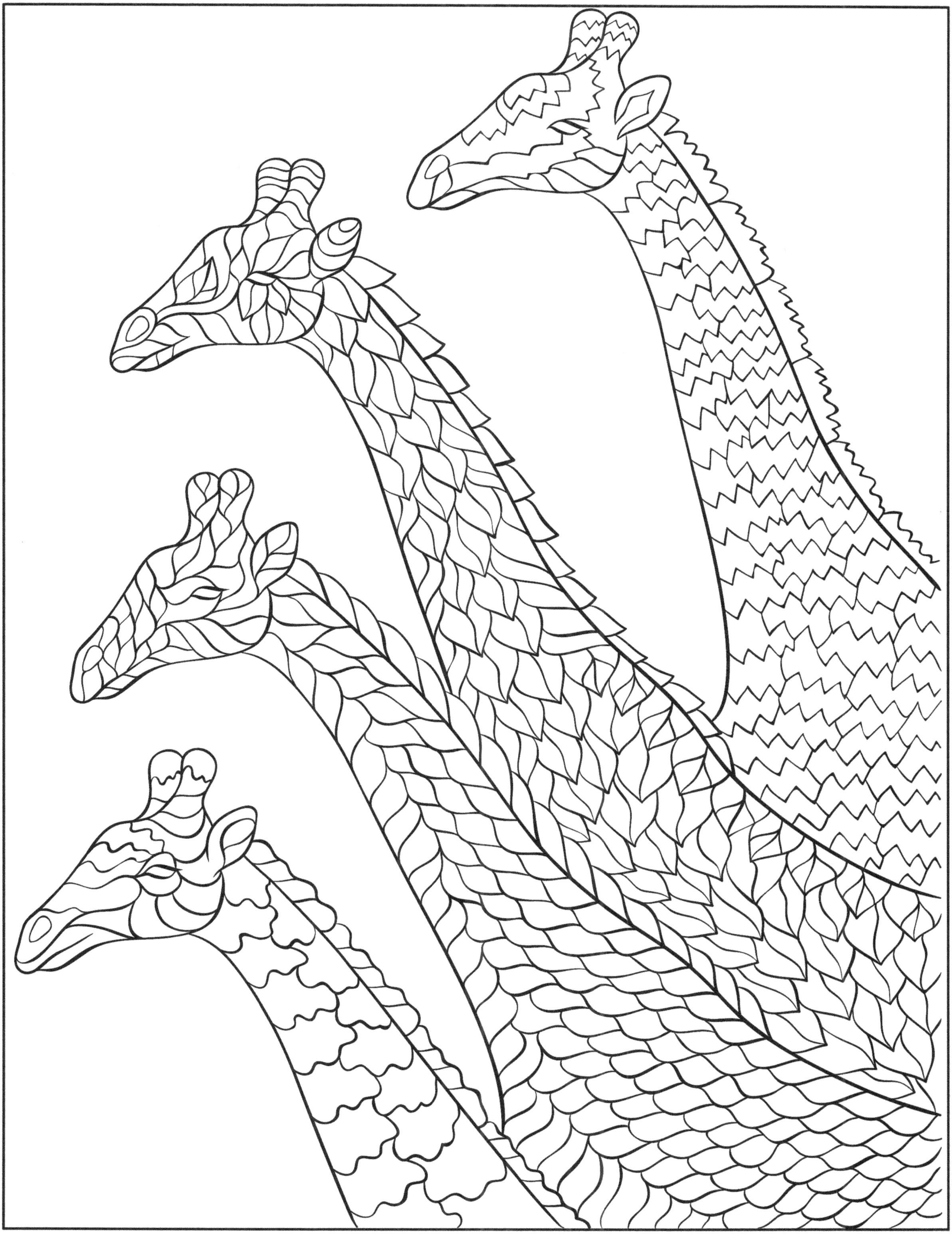

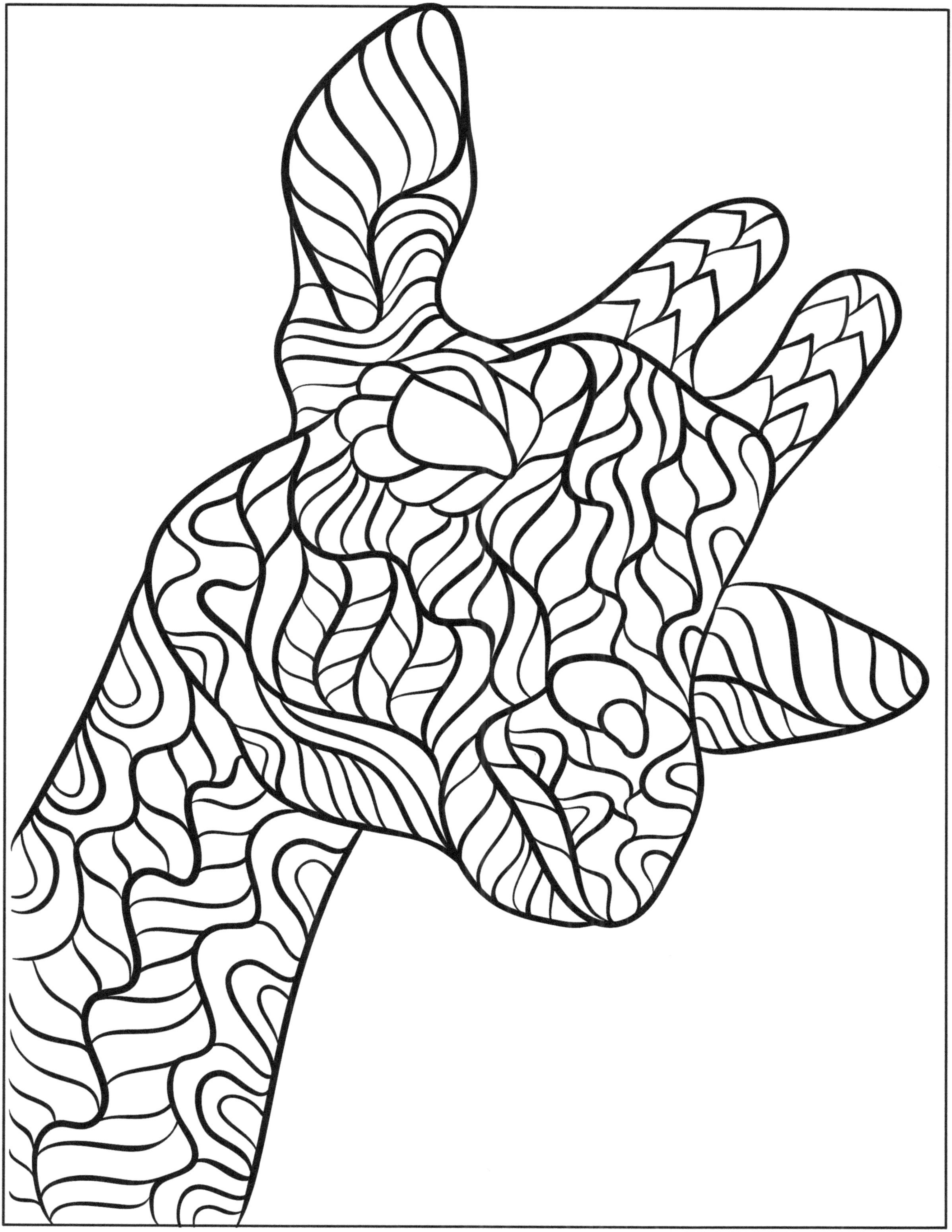

www.ingramcontent.com/pod-product-compliance
Lightning Source LLC
Chambersburg PA
CBHW081148280526
45787CB00008B/3255
* 9 7 8 1 5 4 8 3 0 5 0 8 6 *